CHAMELEONS

LIVING WILD

LIVING WILD

Published by Creative Paperbacks
P.O. Box 227, Mankato, Minnesota 56002
Creative Paperbacks is an imprint of The Creative Company
www.thecreativecompany.us

Design and production by Mary Herrmann
Art direction by Rita Marshall
Printed in the United States of America

Photographs by Alamy (AF archive, Danita Delimont, imagebroker), Dreamstime (Awie Badenhorst, Francois Dreyer, Brian Flaigmore, Hitman1111, Janpietruszka, Mikhail Kusayev, Mgkuijpers, Carlos Soler Martinez, Ben Twist, Zak71), Geoffrey W. Gordon, iStockphoto (Warwick Lister-Kaye), Shutterstock (B & T Media Group Inc., Jessica Bethke, bierchen, Casey K. Bishop, Dja65, Elmarié Dreyer, Sebastian Duda, EcoPrint, Esterio, FikMik, fivespots, Iarus, Eric Isselee, Nagy Jozsef – Attila, kefiiir, Cathy Keifer, Maitree Laipitaksin, Olga Lipatova, Maisna, Stephen Meese, Isabella Pfenninger, Julie Remezova, Robynrg, rook76, Casper Simon), Wikipedia (Steve Evans/flickr, Greg Hume, JialiangGao, Axel Strauss)

Photograph p. 32 by Geoffrey W. Gordon, courtesy of Dr. Martha J. Ehrlich: *Chameleon Staff Finial for a Ruler's Spokesman*, Asante People, Ghana, 20th c.; wood, embossed gold leaf. Height: 7-1/4" (83 mm); length: 5" (127 mm); depth: 2-1/2" (65 mm).

Library of Congress Cataloging-in-Publication Data
Gish, Melissa.
Chameleons / by Melissa Gish.
p. cm. — (Living wild)
Includes index.
Summary: A look at chameleons, including their habitats, physical characteristics such as their color-changing skin, behaviors, relationships with humans, and fragile status in the world today.
ISBN 978-1-60818-285-5 (hardcover)
ISBN 978-0-89812-838-3 (pbk)
1. Chameleons—Juvenile literature. I. Title.

QL666.L23G47 2013
597.95'6—dc23   2012023305

First Edition
9 8 7 6 5 4 3 2 1

CHAMELEONS

Melissa Gish

The sun is rising on a garden in Cape Town, where beads of dew shimmer on the leaves of a honeysuckle bush. A Cape dwarf chameleon watches butterflies flit from one blossom to another.

The sun is rising on a backyard garden in Cape Town, South Africa, where beads of dew shimmer on the leaves of a honeysuckle bush. A Cape dwarf chameleon watches butterflies flit from one bright orange blossom to another as they take in the sweet nectar. They are unaware of the predator hidden among the leaves. The chameleon is motionless, its toes and long tail wrapped firmly around a slender branch. A breeze rustles the leaves, and the chameleon shakes its body back and forth, mimicking the movement of the leaves. It takes the opportunity to lift one foot and step slowly toward one of the blossoms. Standing still, the chameleon waits— but not for long, for a butterfly lands on a flower near the chameleon's face. In a fraction of a second, the chameleon shoots out its tongue, nabs the butterfly, and pulls the helpless creature into its mouth.

WHERE IN THE WORLD THEY LIVE

■ **Jackson's Chameleon**
Kenya and Tanzania

■ **Oustalet's Chameleon**
Madagascar

■ **Common Chameleon**
southern Europe, North Africa, Middle East

■ **Veiled Chameleon**
Yemen, Saudi Arabia, United Arab Emirates

■ **Panther Chameleon**
Madagascar

■ **Brown Leaf Chameleon**
Madagascar

MADAGASCAR

■ **Flap-necked Chameleon**
sub-Saharan Africa

■ **Cape Dwarf Chameleon**
South Africa

The island nation of Madagascar claims more than half of the world's approximately 150 chameleon species. The remaining chameleons are native to other African countries, the Middle East, and parts of southern Europe and western India. The colored squares represent the native locations of eight distinctive chameleon species.

CURIOUS CHAMELEONS

Like many other reptiles, such as tortoises and crocodiles, chameleons and other lizards existed on Earth long before many commonly known dinosaurs appeared. Chameleons are members of the order Squamata, or scaled lizards, which includes not only lizards but also snakes. There are more than 150 species of chameleon distributed among several groups in the subfamilies Chamaeleoninae (chameleons with long, curled tails) and Brookesiinae (chameleons with stubbed or straight tails). The word "chameleon" comes from the ancient Greek words *khamai*, which means "on the ground," and *leon*, which means "lion" and refers to the fierce appearance and voracious appetite of many chameleons.

Chameleons are solitary creatures, inhabiting mostly forested environments. More than half of all chameleon species are found nowhere else but on the island of Madagascar and its neighboring small islands. Other chameleon species are found throughout central and southern Africa, and in moist coastal regions around northern Africa, the Middle East, western India, and Sri Lanka as well as southern Spain and nations surrounding

The rhinoceros chameleon is named for the single horn that protrudes from its nose, which is more prominent in males than in females.

Chameleons can suffer heat stress if their body temperature exceeds 92 °F (33.3 °C).

the Mediterranean Sea. While not native to the United States, escaped or released pet chameleons have been introduced to southern Florida, southern California, and Hawaii, where **feral** populations now exist.

As reptiles, chameleons are ectothermic animals, meaning that their bodies depend on external sources of heat, and their temperatures change with the environment. In the morning and late afternoon, chameleons are most active, warming their bodies in the sun. At midday, when the sun becomes stronger, they retreat to shady areas to prevent overheating. They sleep at night. Most chameleons are oviparous, which means they reproduce by laying eggs that hatch weeks or months after being laid. But some chameleon species are ovoviviparous, which means the young develop in eggs that hatch inside their mothers' bodies and are later born live.

Chameleons have many lizard relatives, but the closest is a group of more than 300 lizards in the family Agamidae, the dragon lizards. The bearded dragon, which is a popular exotic pet, is an example of the chameleon's closest kin. While chameleons vary greatly in size and color, the main difference between the two

The bearded dragon can grow to 24 inches (61 cm), nearly as long as the largest chameleon species.

Madagascan authorities restrict pet traders to exporting no more than 2,000 panther chameleons each year.

chameleon subfamilies can be found by observing their tails. The Chamaeleoninae, whose members are called typical chameleons, have a strong **prehensile** tail. These chameleons use their tail as a fifth limb, straightening it as they walk to provide balance, or curling it like a hand around vegetation for support. Members of the Brookesiinae family are called atypical chameleons. Their tails, unable to curl, are weakly prehensile. Most atypical chameleons' tails are short, which is why they are also called stub-tailed chameleons.

In the wide world of reptiles, chameleons are made distinctive by the protrusions on their head and face, which vary greatly in shape, size, and number among the species. The top part of a chameleon's head that rises above the neck is called the casque, which is a French word meaning "helmet." Casques—typically larger in males than in females—may be barely noticeable in some species, such as the Madagascar forest chameleon, or so large that they even consist of a pair of crests, as in the Oustalet's (or Malagasy giant) chameleon. Some casques double the height of the head, as in the male veiled chameleon of the Middle East. Many chameleons also

Namaqua chameleons dig holes for shade and expel salt from their nasal glands to conserve moisture.

In Tunisia, chameleons are traditionally buried in the foundations of new buildings to protect the inhabitants from bad luck.

Clamp-like toes allow chameleons to remain motionless for hours, though such inactivity can cause dehydration.

have gular crests, which are scaly flaps under the chin. And most male chameleons have protrusions on the tip of the face, usually in front of or on top of the nostrils, which females lack. These protrusions may be short and pointed, as in the carpenter's chameleon, or, as in the case of the strange-horned chameleon of Africa, flat like the end of a Popsicle stick. The Parson's chameleon of Madagascar has two round bulbs on the tip of its face, and the Jackson's chameleon, native to the mountains of Kenya and Tanzania, has three long, sharp horns reminiscent of a triceratops. Jackson's chameleons are also known as three-horned chameleons for this reason.

The chameleon's body is flattened, so at first glance—especially to most predators—it might look like a leaf. Most chameleons have spiny projections on their backs. The hooded chameleon's spines are bumpy ridges; the short-horned chameleon has sharp spines spaced apart by a series of short spikes; and the Cape dwarf chameleon has evenly spaced spikes like a saw blade. A chameleon's feet are unique among reptiles. Chameleons have the typical number of toes—five—on the front feet, but these toes are fused together, with three bundled toes pointing

one way and two bundled toes pointing the opposite direction. This toe arrangement, called zygodactylism, is a trait shared with birds. The back toes are zygodactylous as well, with a pair of two-toe bundles on each foot. The fused toes are strong, providing a firm grip as the chameleon climbs tree trunks and branches in its habitat. Each toe has a sharp claw that helps the chameleon grip tree bark as it climbs.

It was once believed that chameleons were deaf.

The two subspecies of Parson's chameleon are found primarily in northeastern and central-eastern Madagascar.

However, recent research has shown that chameleons hear sounds that are very low pitched. The reason for their having such poor hearing is still unclear to scientists, but chameleons make up for their lack of hearing with excellent eyesight. They are the only reptiles with full 360-degree vision. Each of the chameleon's eyes is covered by a cone-shaped lid with only a small opening in the middle. The eyes can be rotated independently of each other, allowing the chameleon to look in two different directions at once. To see clearly, however, the chameleon must use both eyes to focus and judge distance. Some chameleon species can spot insects from as far away as 17 feet (5.2 m).

Although new species of chameleon are still being discovered, the smallest chameleon yet found is *Brookesia minima*, commonly called the pygmy leaf chameleon or Madagascan dwarf chameleon. It is no more than 1.3 inches (3.3 cm) long. At up to 27 inches (68.6 cm) in length, the Oustalet's chameleon is the largest species. Female chameleons are typically smaller than males. Chameleon coloration varies from browns and greens to yellow, orange, reddish, blue, and even purple.

The claws of wild chameleons wear down naturally, but captive chameleons' may need to be trimmed.

Chameleon scales are heterogeneous, meaning that they are not uniform in shape or size.

RAINBOW LIZARDS

Chameleons are probably best known for their ability to change color. It was once believed that chameleons could change color at will, observing their environment and adjusting their coloration to match in an effort at **camouflage**. However, research has revealed that this is not the case for most chameleons. Adult chameleons are territorial and will defend a hunting area of up to 400 square feet (37 sq m). Animal ecologist Mariano Cuadrado, curator at ZooBotánico in Jerez, Spain, conducted extensive research on chameleon communication and found that color changing is closely tied to territorial defense, social interaction, and mating strategies. Color changing is also an involuntary response to temperature changes in a chameleon's environment. Not all chameleons can change color as dramatically as others. Some can turn only from light brown to dark brown and back again.

The top layer of chameleon skin, called the epidermis, is transparent. Sandwiched between thin layers of skin underneath the epidermis are millions of chromatophores, which are tiny sacs containing red and yellow **pigments**. The deepest layer of skin is covered with special cells

New species of dwarf and pygmy chameleons are still being found in Madagascan rainforests.

The Marshall's pygmy chameleon grows to just three inches (7.6 cm) long and resembles a leaf when standing still.

Madagascar's jewel chameleon can live in a variety of habitats, from moist forests in the wilderness to dry rock gardens in cities.

that reflect blue and white light, and growing out of that layer are strands of a substance called melanin, the same substance that colors human skin. A chameleon's skin changes color when a number of things occur at once: the chromatophores expand or shrink, adjusting the amount of red and yellow; the reflecting cells expand or shrink, adjusting the amount of blue or white that is reflected; and the melanin strands thicken or shrink, adjusting the amount of brown color. And all of these actions can occur simultaneously in a split second, turning a dark green chameleon bright yellow and vice versa.

Scientists are unsure exactly what triggers chameleons' color changing. It could be chemical reactions in the brain or responses related to the central nervous system. Some scientists believe chameleon color is tied to **hormones**. However they do it, chameleons are masters of color changing. Depending on the species, chameleons can be nearly black one moment and bright purple the next, or instantly shift from mottled brown to brilliant red. Chameleons can also make their skin appear spotted or striped, and they can even create patterns such as blocks or diamonds on their skin.

In general, a cold chameleon will be darker than a warm one. Likewise, an angry chameleon will be darker than a content chameleon. In defending a territory, a male chameleon, with his mouth agape, typically darkens his skin, bobs his head up and down, and rocks his body to and fro, communicating his anger at an intruder. While chameleons may fight over territory or mating rights, pushing and biting each other, usually the intensity of color and aggressive gestures are enough to send a smaller,

Most chameleons lose their bright coloration and turn a dull gray when their body temperature drops.

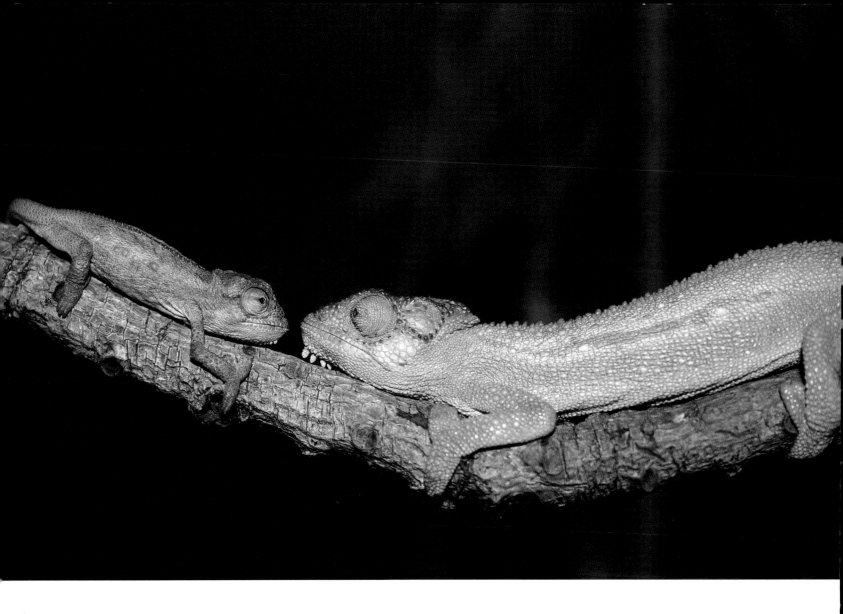

weaker chameleon on its way. Males are particularly
hostile to each other when seeking mates.

For most chameleon species, courtship rituals involve
both color changing and body shaking. Males and females
change color, though females change less dramatically. For
example, the male Cape dwarf chameleon exhibits bright
orange, turquoise blue, white, and lime green, while
the female of that species turns green with white stripes.
Mating usually takes place in summer. It is the only time

of year that chameleons tolerate each other's company.

About 20 species of chameleon spend their entire lives on the ground, hunting insects in leaf litter. The rest rarely leave the trees except to lay eggs, which happens three to six weeks after mating. When an oviparous chameleon is ready to lay eggs, she digs a hole in the earth about twice as deep as she is long and deposits her eggs, called a clutch. The clutch size and **incubation** period vary by species. The ground-dwelling brown leaf chameleon, for example, lays 2 to 5 eggs, which hatch within 70 days. The tree-dwelling panther chameleon lays between 10 and 40 eggs, which must incubate for about 8 months. Ovoviviparous chameleons hold their eggs inside their bodies for five to six months. They expel live young, which are surrounded by soft, gooey **membranes** that they soon squirm out of, fully developed but very small. About 20 percent of chameleon species are ovoviviparous.

Young chameleons, in general, grow quickly. Like all reptiles, chameleons must shed their skin as they grow larger and older because reptilian skin does not stretch and grow as the creature develops. This process typically takes a few days at a time and occurs three or four times a year

When threatened, a short-horned chameleon raises its oversized ear flaps to appear larger and opens its mouth.

Shedding may take several days in areas with high humidity or several weeks if the environment is dry.

Chameleons have been found to be picky eaters, preferring fat, juicy, protein-rich grasshoppers and worms to slenderer, crunchier insect prey.

throughout an adult chameleon's life, as old, dying skin is replaced by new, healthy skin. In some species, young chameleons may reach their full size within a few weeks, and in other species, chameleons take several months to fully develop. Panther chameleons reach maturity at seven months, but many ground-dwelling chameleon species are not fully mature until the age of one or two years. Labord's chameleon of Madagascar reaches maturity within two months of hatching, mates, and then lays eggs within another two months. After reproducing, these chameleons die. Existing for only about five months, the Labord's chameleon holds the record for the shortest life span of any **vertebrate** on the planet. Most chameleons live up to six years, but larger chameleon species tend to live longer. Meller's chameleons, which grow to 21 inches (53.3 cm) in length, can live up to 12 years.

Chameleons are positioned in the middle of the **food chain**, feeding on insects and small vertebrates and providing food for larger animals such as snakes, birds, and small **mammals**. Young chameleons are particularly vulnerable to attack. Even large insects or swarms of ants can turn the tables on chameleons and prey on their

young. Chameleons have a remarkable tongue that makes them successful hunters of hopping and flying insects and, in the case of large chameleons, birds and lizards. The tongue, which is about one and a half times as long as the chameleon's body, is anchored around a slender bone that is shot forward out of the mouth, launching the tongue at high speed. The tip of the tongue is a bulbous suction cup covered with sticky mucus. Once the tongue tip hooks its target, the tongue is instantly retracted, pulling the prey into the chameleon's mouth, where powerful jaws crush it. Unlike other lizards, chameleons chew their food, using the tiny teeth that line their jaws.

The powerful sticking quality of the chameleon's tongue makes prey's escape virtually impossible.

The natural colorfulness of chameleons even inspires fountains decorated by small colored pieces of stone or glass.

DEMONS AND DRAGONS

T he chameleon is part of the traditions and **mythology** of many African **cultures**. According to some myths, the chameleon is a protector. The Fon people of Benin and western Nigeria tell how the two-headed god Mawu-Lisa, creator of the sun and the moon, sent a chameleon to protect the first people in the world. The chameleon's changing skin worked like a mirror, showing the people when danger approached from behind their backs. The Mensa people, a nomadic tribe traditionally from the area now called Eritrea on the coast of the Red Sea, believed that the chameleon had healing power. A chameleon would be placed on the head or body of a person with an ailment. When the chameleon changed color, it meant the chameleon had absorbed the illness into its own body. The chameleon was then discarded, taking the person's sickness or pain with it.

Despite being shy, harmless creatures, chameleons carry a bad reputation in some of their native lands. Their spiked, horned, color-changing appearance is considered magical, and their bulging eyes, demonic. People in northern Africa believe chameleons to be bad luck and may kill chameleons

Unlike the 100 species of their gecko relatives, chameleons cannot re-grow their tails if they are damaged or broken off.

Chameleons have tender skin that can easily be burned if the animal stands on a hot surface for too long.

on sight, even today. A myth from the Swahili people, native to coastal Kenya, Tanzania, and Mozambique, tells how the chameleon came to be loathed by the Swahili. The creator of all things, called the Old Old One, sent the chameleon on an errand to tell humans that the Old Old One would promise them immortality, meaning they would never die. The chameleon set off for the village of men, but he was slow and soon stopped to rest and eat some berries. Time passed, and the chameleon fell asleep. The Old Old One, having had time to think about his promise, decided it was better to let humans live only a short time. He sent the lizard to the village of men to tell them that they could not be immortal and would have to eventually die. The lizard ran swiftly and delivered the message. When the chameleon finally arrived at the village, the humans became angry, saying, "If you had hurried, we would have had the Old Old One's promise of immortality, but since you delayed, we must be mortal." This is why in Swahili tradition, the chameleon is a despised creature, and finding one inside a person's home is considered bad luck.

According to a creation myth of the Yao people of northern Mozambique, only the god Mulungu and the animals inhabited the world in the early days. All the creatures were peaceful, and life was calm. One day, Chameleon made a fish net and cast it into the river. He pulled up two small creatures he had never seen before. He took them to Mulungu, who told Chameleon that he had found man and woman. He instructed Chameleon to set them free and let them grow, which Chameleon did. But man and woman eventually made fire and began to eat the animals. This destruction cast fear into the hearts of the animals, who retreated into the forest. Chameleon climbed high into the treetops, where he remains today, trembling with fear and darkening his skin whenever he sees a human.

In the storytelling tradition of the Ashanti people of Ghana, Chameleon is at times a trickster. Spider

Chameleons and other wildlife still play important symbolic roles in the rituals of the Yao people.

In Ashanti art, the chameleon is always shown with its tail curved unnaturally upward instead of down.

wagered with Chameleon one day, and by cheating he acquired all Chameleon's grain. For revenge, Chameleon made a fancy coat of woven vines and decorated it with shiny flies. He flaunted it around Spider, who begged Chameleon to hand it over to him. Chameleon said he would sell it to Spider. He wanted only enough grain to fill the small hole in his storehouse. Spider agreed, and he sent two daughters to Chameleon's storehouse with grain. But Chameleon had dug a deep pit under the storehouse. Spider's daughters made many trips to fill the hole, eventually delivering all the grain to Chameleon in exchange for the coat, which had dried up and turned ugly by then. This is why chameleons are always smiling and spiders hide in corners, too embarrassed to be seen.

More contemporary stories of chameleons depict them as shy, even nervous creatures. Emily Gravett's 2011 book, *Blue Chameleon*, features a title character who is timid and lonely. The 2011 animated movie *Rango* tells the story of a jittery pet chameleon who finds himself accidentally stranded in a Mojave Desert town called Dirt after his owners lose him. Despite a number of horrifying events, including being attacked by a hawk

and terrorized by a rattlesnake, Rango, voice-acted by Johnny Depp, finds courage and uses his color-changing chameleon talents and a newly discovered sense of pride to become the town's hero.

Chameleons can be found in other animated forms as well. Espio the Chameleon appears in several of Sonic the Hedgehog's video games and comic books. Trained as a ninja, the purple reptile with a curly tail and a yellow horn has the ability to become invisible and move around undetected. He can also crawl on walls and ceilings, and can destroy most opponents by smashing

Rango, directed by Gore Verbinski, won the Academy Award for best Animated Feature Film in 2012.

The Jackson's chameleon was named in 1896 for Frederick John Jackson, then governor of Kenya.

into them. In the world of Pokémon, Charmeleon is the chameleon-like middle stage of an **evolving** reptile character, the first stage being Charmander, a salamander, and the last being Charizard, a dragon lizard. Charmeleon is bright orange with a flaming tail. He can breathe fire and uses his powerful tail to attack opponents. Comic book collectors know the character Chameleon from the Marvel Universe. Though not a true reptile, Chameleon is a master of disguise and an evil nemesis of Daredevil, Spider-Man, Iron Man, and other Marvel heroes.

Stamp collectors find that chameleons are popular on postage stamps around the world, too. A variety of chameleons have appeared on stamps from Ghana, South Africa, Zaire, Namibia, Vietnam, Malta, and many other nations. Burkina Faso and Sierra Leone issued stamps depicting the flap-necked chameleon; the Jackson's chameleon appeared on stamps from Belgium and the Democratic Republic of the Congo; and France issued a stamp with the image of a reunion chameleon. In 1973, Madagascar's jewel and big-nosed chameleons appeared on stamps from their native country.

Most captive chameleon species can live up to seven or eight years, given proper dietary and environmental conditions.

Herpetologists around the world consider the decline of chameleons in Africa and Madagascar a serious ecological issue. These reptiles suffer from habitat loss and from exploitation for the **commercial** pet trade. Because chameleons are slow moving, they cannot escape the chainsaws and bulldozers used by loggers, and they are easy targets for people who capture them and their young to sell as pets. Some countries, such as Kenya and South Africa, have banned the exportation of chameleons for the pet trade, and other countries closely regulate the sale of chameleons. However, the increasing demand for exotic pets, including chameleons, has fostered a growing black market for wild animals.

Exotic animal trade in the European Union, Japan, and the U.S. is regulated by the Convention on International Trade in Endangered Species of Wild Fauna and Flora (CITES). Countries not affiliated with CITES are not regulated, so groups such as the World Wildlife Fund (WWF) and TRAFFIC, which is an animal trade monitoring network that was established in 1976, investigate and prosecute illegal activities involving the

Issued in 1973, this stamp of a jewel chameleon was one of many such stamps produced in Madagascar.

Chameleons prefer calm, quiet habitats, and those kept as pets in noisy or high-activity areas often get highly stressed and become ill.

Deforestation is generally considered to be the greatest threat posed to most chameleon species around the globe.

capture and sale of wild plants and animals around the world. TRAFFIC reported that more than 40 percent of Madagascar's reptiles are currently in danger of **extinction**. Chameleons top the list of animals being monitored by TRAFFIC. One species of particular concern is the Tarzan's chameleon, first discovered in 2009 and already listed as critically endangered.

The United Nations Environment Programme–World Conservation Monitoring Centre (UNEP–WCMC) is an organization that provides information to TRAFFIC and other organizations on species and habitats. UNEP–WCMC reported that, from 1993 to 1998, more than 250,000 chameleons were exported from Africa, Yemen, and Seychelles (a nation composed of 115 islands north of Madagascar), and more than 226,000 chameleons were exported from Madagascar. In the U.S., pet chameleons can cost anywhere from $20 for Senegal or leaf chameleons to more than $400 for panther chameleons. Many pet chameleons are **captive-reared** specimens, but too often, wild chameleons are captured and removed from their natural habitats, smuggled aboard planes and ships bound for North America, and end up in the hands of inexperienced pet owners who cannot properly care for them. The trafficking of exotic animals is not a **sustainable** industry, and its impact on a variety of animals—not just chameleons—around the world can be devastating. The best way to stop the exotic pet trade is for people to refuse to buy exotic pets. Without the demand for chameleons, the black market trade in chameleons would cease to exist.

Perhaps an even greater threat to chameleons is the destruction and alteration of their natural habitats. The Smith's dwarf chameleon, found only in a tiny coastal area of South Africa, is one of the few chameleons able to change its color for camouflage. In 1993, to raise awareness for chameleon conservation, the South African government issued a postage stamp commemorating the Smith's dwarf chameleon, which was listed as vulnerable on the Red List

During the dry season in Yemen, veiled chameleons eat leaves to get the moisture they would otherwise receive from rain.

Tanzania's coffee plantations provide inviting habitats for many of East Africa's chameleon species.

of Threatened Species that is published annually by the International Union for Conservation of Nature (IUCN). Despite such efforts to increase visibility, however, this species continued to decline, and three years later its IUCN rating was changed to critically endangered.

In many underdeveloped countries, trees provide the only means of fuel for cooking and heating. Forests are also cut down to make grazing land for cattle and fields for growing crops. Some crops, such as mango, avocado, cocoa, and coffee, provide habitat for chameleons, but when these crops are harvested, the habitat is once again disturbed and many chameleons are forced out or killed. Many chameleon species cannot survive in altered environments such as farmland or orchards because their needs are specifically tied to their natural rainforest habitats. The bizarre-nosed chameleon, which exists in fragmented areas of northern Madagascar that add up to no more than 39 square miles (101 sq km), is threatened by logging, slash-and-burn agriculture (the practice of cutting trees, burning the land, and digging up the soil for crops), and cattle grazing. It is one of Madagascar's most at-risk chameleon species.

Despite such challenges, some chameleons persist in

the deepest reaches of the Madagascan rainforests. Eleven new species of chameleon have been discovered since 1999, including *Furcifer timoni*, a blue-speckled, white-lipped chameleon that has not yet been given a common name. New populations of species facing extinction are also being discovered, thanks to increased research on the habitats and behaviors of these elusive reptiles. In 2011, conservationists from England's University of Kent discovered a small population of the Belalanda chameleon, previously known to exist in only two isolated coastal areas of southwestern Madagascar. One of the world's rarest reptiles, the Belalanda chameleon is now the target of intensive conservation efforts led by the Darwin Initiative, WWF, and the IUCN Chameleon Specialist Group.

Research on the **genetic** makeup of chameleon populations may be helpful in conservation efforts. The Reptile Speciation Project, headquartered in South Africa, aims to study the **DNA** of chameleons to determine how chameleon populations adjust to changes in their habitat. The research group is also involved in classifying and recording information about new chameleon species and subspecies that are discovered. Researchers study wild

Like many chameleons, the Owen's chameleon of western Africa falls to the ground, pretending to be a dry leaf, when it is threatened.

Panther chameleons of northwestern Madagascar and the nearby island of Nosy Be are usually bright blue in color.

chameleons by recording their behavior, capturing them, marking them with numbers and taking their pictures, and then releasing them. When chameleons are recaptured, information on their movements and behaviors is recorded. In this way, chameleon movements, behaviors, and survival can be tracked over a period of days, weeks, or months. Researchers also study how chameleons respond to habitat changes by taking blood samples and analyzing chameleons' stress hormones. Such data can help scientists and conservationists create protection methods and plans for specific chameleon habitats.

Chameleons are precious jewels of the rainforest, yet they are being driven to extinction. Some species are being relocated to protected areas, and tree-planting programs have been initiated in certain habitats, but it may be too late for many chameleon species. While some chameleon species thrive in remote areas, and some survive in habitats despite human interaction, many small, fragile populations of chameleons are at high risk of extinction in their present locations. If serious conservation measures are not undertaken, much of the amazing variety of chameleons could disappear from our planet forever.

A wild carpet chameleon has a life span of about 18 months, but captive-raised individuals have been known to survive more than 3 years.

ANIMAL TALE: THE CURSE OF CHAMELEON

Animals play a major role in the folklore of virtually every culture on Earth. The same can be said of chameleons in Africa. In this folk tale from the Zulu people of southern Africa, the chameleon is a messenger who reveals why chameleons now move so slowly.

Long ago, after the Creator had finished making the world and all its creatures, one thing troubled him: the first man and woman were starting to look old and worn. He wanted to keep them looking young and beautiful, so he created a gift that would restore their fine features.

To bestow this gift upon the humans, he called on Chameleon, the swiftest runner on Earth. "Chameleon," commanded the Creator, "take this package with great haste to the people."

"Certainly," replied Chameleon. He took from the Creator a bundle wrapped in fresh oak leaves and tied tightly with a stem of grass. "I will not fail you," called Chameleon over his shoulder as he dashed away as swift as the wind.

The journey to the village of the people was a long one, and Chameleon grew thirsty. He stopped at the river for a drink of water. Snake was drinking from the river, too. "Hello, Chameleon," said Snake. "You seem to be in a great hurry. Where are you going?"

"I must deliver a gift for the people from the Creator," replied Chameleon.

"Ah," said Snake, nodding. Snake hated the people. He was jealous of the special treatment they received from the Creator.

"I must go now," said Chameleon. "It was nice to see you."

"Wait!" cried Snake. "We are cousins, and my family has missed you. Please come share a meal with us today."

"I cannot," said Chameleon. "I must hurry to the village."

"Well," said Snake, "one might think you are too good to visit with your relatives despite your being so close by."

"Oh, no," said Chameleon, "I meant no offense. I will come visit for a while. I can still get to the people's village before sundown."

"Splendid!" cried Snake. "Follow me." And with that, Snake led Chameleon off to his family's burrow.

Chameleon shared a fabulous meal with Snake and his family. But Snake's jealousy simmered beneath the surface of his friendly conversation. He served Chameleon *utshwala* (*OO-chwah-lah*), which is a traditional Zulu beverage with intoxicating effects. Soon Chameleon's head nodded and his eyelids drooped. Forgetting all about his delivery, Chameleon fell asleep. Snake laughed.

"What is so funny?" Snake's wife asked.

"Look here," said Snake, lifting the package from the floor where Chameleon had set it. He tore open the package. "New skins!" Snake exclaimed. "The Creator sent the people new skins, but they're ours now."

The commotion woke Chameleon, who watched in horror as Snake and his wife slipped into the new skins meant for the people. "You musn't!" he cried. "The Creator will punish me!"

"Too bad," said Snake. "These belong to us now." And he slithered away with his wife.

Chameleon felt so ashamed at his failure that he ran away to the forest and hid in the trees. To this day, he creeps slowly over branches and stands rigid like a leaf to hide from the Creator. And Snake looks young because he is able to shed his skin and don a new one every year.

GLOSSARY

camouflage – the ability to hide, due to coloring or markings that blend in with a given environment

captive-reared – raised in a place from which escape is not possible

commercial – suitable for business and to gain a profit rather than for personal reasons

cultures – particular groups in a society that share behaviors and characteristics that are accepted as normal by that group

DNA – deoxyribonucleic acid, a substance found in every living thing that determines the species and individual characteristics of that thing

estivates – slows down the body systems and sleeps without food or water

evolving – gradually developing into a new form

extinction – the act or process of becoming extinct; coming to an end or dying out

feral – in a wild state after having been domesticated

food chain – a system in nature in which living things are dependent on each other for food

genetic – relating to genes, the basic physical units of heredity

herpetologists – people who study reptiles and their lives

hormones – chemical substances produced in the body that control and regulate the activity of certain cells and organs

incubation – keeping an egg warm and protected until it is time for it to hatch

mammals – warm-blooded animals that have a backbone and hair or fur, give birth to live young, and produce milk to feed their young

membranes – thin, clear layers of tissue that cover an internal organ or developing organism

mythology – a collection of myths, or popular, traditional beliefs or stories that explain how something came to be or that are associated with a person or object

pigments – materials or substances present in the tissues of animals or plants that give them their natural coloring

prehensile – capable of grasping

sustainable – able to be renewed or kept functioning

vertebrate – an animal that has a backbone, including mammals, birds, reptiles, amphibians, and fish

SELECTED BIBLIOGRAPHY

ARKive. "Parson's Chameleon (*Calumma parsonii*)." http://www.arkive.org/parsons-chameleon/calumma-parsonii/.

Badger, David. *Lizards: A Natural History of Some Uncommon Creatures—Extraordinary Chameleons, Iguanas, Geckos, & More*. Stillwater, Minn.: Voyageur Press, 2002.

Le Berre, François. *The Chameleon Handbook*. Hauppauge, N.Y.: Barron's, 2009.

Mattison, Chris. *Firefly Encyclopedia of Reptiles and Amphibians*. 2nd ed. Buffalo, N.Y.: Firefly Books, 2008.

San Diego Zoo. "Animal Bytes: Chameleons." http://www.sandiegozoo.org/animalbytes/t-chameleon.html.

Tolley, Krystal, and Marius Burger. *Chameleons of Southern Africa*. Cape Town: Struik Nature, 2007.

Despite human encroachment, many chameleon species can adapt quickly to changing environmental conditions.

INDEX